What's Next
Thoughts On What Happens After We Die

By

Allen C. Liles
Liles Communications, LLC

What's Next
Thoughts On What Happens After We Die

by

Allen C. Liles
Liles Communications, LLC

Published By
Positive Imaging, LLC
bill@positive-imaging.com

ISBN: 9781951776947

These personal thoughts are dedicated to the dear souls contemplating the ultimate journey. May your transition be peaceful and full of positivity for the next adventure.

A special thank you to my publisher A. William Benitez for his treasured insight and generosity.

Contents

THE COMING JOURNEY

In February 2021, 1 was a retired minister that had just been diagnosed with Stage 4 prostate cancer. The urologist performing the biopsy told me: "I'm sorry. It's a very aggressive form. You might want to begin your radiology treatments next week." I explained to the doc, "I have already thought about the possibility of cancer. I'm nearly 85 years old. I've had a great life. I've decided to opt for quality of life and skip any treatments. By the way, what is your best guess about the time remaining?" He stroked his beard and answered: "One year, maybe two".

Now, over two years later, I am still around. But my physical condition tells me that things have gone downhill over the past two months. It won't be long before I move forward to the next stop on my spiritual journey. As an ordained minister, this precious time between diagnosis and end stage has caused me to think about "What's Next?" Of course, I already have some preconceived notions. My ministerial path encourages a more metaphysical approach to questions of the spirit. I have prayed and meditated often about the subject. I meditate daily, usually in the early morning. Spending time in the silence has helped my spiritual consciousness to advance. I constantly ask The Holy Spirit that I know lives within me (John 14: 26) about "eternity." I listen to my own inner voice aided by years of studying scripture. I have even paid attention to what I perceive are the celestial musings of my dearly departed wife, Jan Carmen Liles. She passed from a sudden heart attack on Feb. 28, 2017. 1 believe the souls of our loved ones are still around, eager to teach and guide us. From each of these sources, I have received some startling insights about the afterlife. However, I do not claim any mystical gifts. Perhaps my religious orientation has created a higher awareness of spiritual possibilities. Mainly I want to offer every one of you an optimistic view of "What's Next?". All I ask is a willingness to be open and receptive to new thinking about the afterlife. If nothing else, my benign view might reduce the fearfulness that overwhelms so many of us near the end. I would also reiterate that these perceptions are not theological, philosophical, scholarly or scientific. There are many fine books and articles with well-reasoned and learned predictions and conclusions. This is not one of them. I am just offering one person's opinion, which may strike some as a fantasy of sorts. To me, it seems very real. Here is the bottom line for me: I no longer fear death. I have a deep belief that what comes next is far better than what we have now. Yes, I hope my final moments on earth are not painful or lingering. I also would appreciate my departure flowing with as little commotion as possible. My 67-year-old father experienced a fatal heart attack in the express lane of the local Safeway store.in 1979. Now that caused a big-time stir. Other than those low-key wishes, I am anticipating the upcoming adventure. It looks promising. For example, I believe the first thing we notice in our crossing over will be the beautiful rainbows. As we depart our earthly form for the final time, I see us beholding an overwhelming convergence of rainbows. This may later seem contradictory. The only real complaint ever heard about Heaven from new arrivals concerns rain. Since all days in eternity remain forever flawless, there is no need for rain. Former human souls seem to miss an occasional shower or good old-fashioned thunderstorm.

What happens when we are transported to eternity? I believe our individual souls are first lifted out of the now useless shell known as the physical body. We leave behind whatever form we used to travel the earth. We are no longer tall or short, stout or thin. We have no further need for flesh and bones. All that remains is the original soul that traveled with us down from Heaven to this parenthesis on earth. We are returning intact to the place where we originated. I believe we first travel down a tunnel toward a distant light. Or, in my case, I visualize my soul riding in a noiseless glider, high above an ever-receding planet. I am the only passenger. My airship is being piloted by an angelic captain, responsible for a safe arrival at the portals of God's Kingdom. It seems like a smooth flight. The lights of earth begin to dim and then disappear. We travel along in quiet darkness for a brief time. Then I envision the gates of Heaven rising before us. As we approach our destination, the entrance to "Eternity" opens. My personal glider lands without a bump. I turn with gratitude to thank my pilot, but he has already disappeared. More work to do, I guess.

As I deplane, I am awed by several things. There is profound color and beauty in every direction. It is as though I have stepped into a masterful work of art. But I am mostly amazed at the huge crowd of souls that await my arrival. What is going on here? In the forefront are my sweet mother Edith (gone now for half a century) and dear wife Jan. I feel their unconditional love, just like on earth. However, it now seems magnified ten thousand times. I feel embraced, accepted, and honored by their presence. But there are so many other souls, all seeking to greet me at the exact moment of arrival. I detect that everybody gathered to welcome me feels a deep affection. I detect no negative opinions being offered about my earthly life. My human father is there, but not in the front ranks. My daddy is standing next to my sister, his personal favorite in our small human family of origin. Oh well, she was kind of amazing. My grandparents on my dad's side are there, as are my Uncle "Johnny" and his wife Aunt "Bunkie". They were always a rowdy couple, and I liked them. I am especially astounded by the wide collection of friends from every section of my human

history. I recognize congregants from every
church we served. I can see Mike and Charlie,
two of my best friends from high school. Waving
at me are Lou and Gage, a couple of college
roommates from my days at Baylor University in
Waco, TX. I see Dan, my best buddy from a long
career in the corporate world. He is gathered
next to a collection of souls from the Dallas advertising business. My boss, the genius that in-
vented Slurpee for 7-Eleven is smiling at me,
along with several souls from the company's in-
house advertising group that bore his name, in
the middle of this collection, I see the agency art
director "Boone" and our mutual copywriter
friend "Peck'. Peck is the guy that thought up the
iconic "Big Gulp" name plus the "Hot to Go" des-
ignation for 7-Eleven's fast-food line. I look further and see some of my ministerial classmates
and associates from my second human career of
ministry. There is crusty old Marcella who went
from a staid corporate banker in Minnesota to a
cantankerous minister. The seminary professors
disliked her independent thinking. Then, I spy
another group that worked with me in our religious denomination's outreach/Marketing De-
partment. There is talented musician "*Coco*", the
Puerto Rico-born audio/visual director. I see
"Michael", our much under-appreciated book editor. I also spy the soul of "Janet", the denomination's magazine editor. She was a talented young
minister who had died in a head-on car accident
immediately after performing a memorial service
for someone else. More than a few of my classmates from the seminary are visible, all waving

encouragement and welcome. Again, there is a total absence of negativity. There are no frowning faces. Everything is 100% positive. The one recent soul not visible is my 54-year-old stepdaughter "Danielle". She had passed without warning the year before. Her mother Jan could tell that I was looking for any sign of Dani. "She's not here; ' Jan's soul informed me. "Danielle never expected to die when she did. When she arrived here, Heaven stunned her. You know that my daughter was always restless. She moved around constantly, from one career to another. The vastness and beauty of God's Kingdom simply overwhelmed her. She could not wait to begin taking it all in. She gathered up her angel wings, said, "I will see you later," and flew away to start exploring. I haven't seen her since, but I know she will be back to love on us both."

I was so glad to see Edith, my sweet mother. Because of her deep faith and Southern Baptist love for God's only son, I was chosen for spiritual service. What a blessing my mother's devotion modeled for me as I became an ordained minister. I could always feel her encouragement as I shifted to a totally new career. As far as I know, my daddy never darkened the door of any church. If it wasn't Democratic politics, the Santa Fe Railroad, or the stock market, he possessed no interest. He just got out of Mother's way when it came to religion. I thanked her again for guiding my spiritual journey. Then she told me one of the most profound truths about our soul's individual journey. "God planned everything before your soul ever showed up on earth in its current form. He orchestrated each part of your life journey, starting back many centuries. Every incarnation advanced the plot. There are no accidents in God's Universe. Nothing is left to chance. Yes, you do possess Free Will. But that only goes so far. It can always be adjusted and often is. When Spirit has a plan for you, nothing gets in the way."

I became aware of a half dozen or so winged creatures crowding around us. "Who are they?" I asked my mother's soul. "They are a few of your Guardian Angels," she told me. "You've had hundreds along the way, but these are the ones that have been the most involved with you. They just wanted to stop by and say hello." She introduced one as the "Angel of Transformation", which made sense since I switched careers in mid-life. Another Mother's soul referred to as a "Celestial Scribe", a nod to my prolific journaling. "Here is one you really challenged on occasion, the Angel of Forgiveness," she said with good humor. "You won't be having any forgiveness problems going forward. There is nothing to forgive here."

Suddenly, I sensed a path being cleared next to my entourage of greeters. "God is stopping by the say hello," Jan's soul whispered. "Don't get too flattered. Spirit greets everyone when they first arrive. God especially loves small babies." With that, I heard and felt a perceptible "whoosh" of movement. I did not visually see anything, but I felt the warmest embrace I had ever known. I felt accepted, loved, lifted, and cleansed. Then, I discerned these specific words: "This is My beloved son, in whom I AM well pleased." Then, the "whoosh" dissipated and disappeared into the ethers of eternity. But I had no doubt. I had just felt the divine Presence of God Itself.

REFLECTIONS ON DYING

We all must deal with physical death. Human forms are pre-destined to vacate their spaces on the planet. Newer and younger bodies wait to slip into the old territory that we once filled. So how should we react? Do we face the coming reality with wondrous expectation, total dread, grudging acceptance or simply by declining to even think about it? It is our individual choice. Every person has her or her own perspective about dying. Some may see it as quite desirable to the physical or mental misery they now face. Others cling to life with a powerful ferocity and determination. The choice can often be murky. One's opinion about living or dying remains forever personal and subject to rapid change. The loss of a loved one or job, an unexpected medical diagnosis or even going broke can shift an opinion about the value of human life. However, most young people cannot conceive of not being around somewhere on the planet. Choosing to give up their life force too early remains unthinkable. Physical death is something that happens to Grammy, Grandpa, and their friends.

Dying is the ultimate example of losing control. We humans crave the ability to control the people, places, and things around us. However, maintaining control over anything or anybody qualifies as a cruel illusion. Nothing ever stays the same for long. The stage is constantly turning over with new plots. Characters come and go. Trying to establish even a semblance of control over people and events quickly becomes frustrating_ The "Serenity Prayer" in the 12-step programs says it best: "God, help me to accept the things I cannot change, the courage to change the things I can and the wisdom to know the difference."

I was senior minister at the Unity Church of Sun City, AZ in the mid 1990s. The average age of our congregation was 83. Illness, death and dying was a common factor. One day, I had a visit from a woman who seemed distressed over her 88-year-old sister. She told me that "Merle" had been in hospice care for more than six months. "She won't die," the lady said. "The hospice team is ready to send her back into the regular system. I don't know what to do. She should have passed months ago. Would you go visit her?" I agreed to see the lady. I meditated about what I should say to her. I believe The Holy Spirit within me provided this guidance: "Merle is afraid about what comes next after she dies. She is worried about going to hell for something that happened during her human life. Please reassure her." That was it. No details. The next day, I entered Merle's dark bedroom. She had a fearful look on her face. Having a preacher come to visit probably did not help. I started out by saying that I was there on behalf of those who cared about her. I reached out and asked if I could take her hand. She lifted it up for me. As I took her wrinkled old hand, I said, "Merle, God wanted me to give you a message. Nothing that you have ever said, done, or been in your life will keep God from welcoming you into Heaven. God loves you. He is waiting for you now with open arms. When you are ready to go, the Angels will come and take you to Heaven. It will be such a happy and wonderful day. I see many rainbows in your future." She did not answer me, but I detected a slight smile. I said a short prayer and left the room. About 3 p.m. the next day, I received a grateful call from Merle's sister. "I don't know what you said, but she passed this morning. The hospice nurse said it was unexpected, but very peaceful." I believe that Merle wanted to hear that God was waiting to welcome her into Heaven. I just happened to be the grateful conduit for that message.

Most people make their transition to the Kingdom of God at the end of a long life, numbering 75 or more years. By that time, many have experienced severe health challenges. This makes the willingness to let go of human life more of a preferable choice. How often have you heard it said about a recently departed person: "Well, at least he (or she) is out of their pain and suffering?" There is a discernible Truth to that opinion. Nobody likes to witness human angst and/or feelings of helplessness and discomfort. I believe one of the instant joys of Transition is that all physical pain disappears forever. Those who struggled to walk now fly through the limitless halls of Heaven unfettered. One of my most common dreams lately has involved "flying". In one specific scenario, I was in an engineless glider soaring silently above a forest. Eventually, the craft touched down in a clearing. I climbed out and looked around. A few yards away, I spied a picnic table. There was a bearded figure in a white robe sitting there, as if waiting for my arrival. I saw him smile and beckon for me to join him. As I approached the table, I beheld a man resembling Jesus the Christ. He extended His hand. We greeted each other warmly. He stood and embraced me in a brother-to-brother fashion. I felt recognized, appreciated, cherished, and loved. We chatted like old friends. Then, he took me by the hand. We began walking out of the clearing and straight into the most beautiful rainbow I had ever seen. I was then released back into the mortal world and on my way home.

Have you ever considered what Heaven might be like? Do you wonder if God will be waiting to personally greet you? Is someone there to hand you a tailored white robe, in your perfect size? How will you spend your first night away from the familiar confines of earth? So many questions, so few answers.

CONFIRMATION OF DANIELLE'S STORY

In 2022, my beautiful stepdaughter Danielle passed unexpectedly. Dani was 54 and full of life. She had just started a home decorating business. It was thriving and new clients were arriving, all eager for Dani's unique creative touch. Emme, the youngest of her three children, had just graduated from high school. Jack, one of her two boys, was already a college graduate. Harry, the youngest son, was enrolled at the state university. Dani's husband (Darren) held an important job with an internationally known corporation. Life was flowing smoothly along. It was all blue skies and green lights.

Then Danielle began having vision problems. Severe headaches appeared. Her doctor suggested that she go to the ER of a local trauma center. As Dani was undergoing a routine procedure, she experienced an aneurism. The doctors placed her in an induced coma state, but she never woke up. In just a few more days, Dani's loving family opted to release her soul to

God's care. The unexpected passing blindsided everyone.

The next day, still in a state of shock myself, I meditated. I asked The Holy Spirit within me if I might have a word with my dear wife Jan's spirit. As Dani's mom, I wondered how she felt about these unforeseen events. I felt Jan's immediate soul presence. "What about Dani's passing?", I asked. "Have you seen her?" I distinctly heard this response: "Just for a few brief seconds, " she replied. "Dani's soul is still in a state of shock. She never expected that this could happen—never in a million years. You know Dani. She is constantly on the go, full of work, activities, her family and life in general. She was a girl that always pursued constant movement and change in her life. In many ways, she was 'restless, irritable and discontent'". The vastness and diversity of Heaven overwhelmed her at first. Then, my restless daughter took off to check things out. As she literally flew away at top speed, the last thing I heard was: "I will see you later, mom." Right now, Dani is still out there exploring. She does not comprehend the vast scope of eternity. Time means nothing here. There will be many eons for her to search every nook and cranny of Heaven. Right now, she is busy soaking it all in. I am sure she'll be back. We shared too much together on the human scene. As you know, Danielle was my youngest child. We developed an incredible bond. I'm just waiting for her to take a breath."

One of the most interesting aspects of the "crossover" into eternity involves "escorts". My wife Jan's father ('Jim") died in 1995 from the effects of a stroke. He was 85. About two weeks prior to his passing, Jim reported seeing a vision of his late mother standing at the foot of his bed. She had been gone for 25 years. The "form" was beckoning for him to join her, presumably on the other side. The experience unsettled Jim. Family members tried to reassure him that it was all a dream. The explanation seemed plausible. Jim relaxed and then, two weeks later, made his own transition.

My cleaning professional "Debra" and her husband "Kenneth" have visited my apartment every two weeks since I moved back to Texas six years ago. They went on a cruise together on Christmas of 2022. After they returned, Kenneth began experiencing some discomfort. One day, he excused himself from dinner, complaining about not feeling well. He headed for the bedroom to lie down. After a few minutes, Debra decided to check on him. Kenneth had his eyes closed, so she assumed he was sleeping. As she backed out of the bedroom, Kenneth bolted straight up in bed with a definite look of fear on his face. He shouted to something in the room: "Are you trying to scare me to death?" Within only a few minutes, he was gone from a massive heart attack. A few weeks later, during one of our regular cleaning appointments, a thought occurred to me. I asked Debra if maybe Kenneth had somehow perceived the presence of a departed loved one. "I do," she told me. "I believe he saw someone that should not have been there." Of course, who really knows what happens a few seconds before death? Supposedly, just a few breaths before he passed, Apple's Steve Jobs called out: "Wow, oh **WOW!** '

Of course, no one knows for sure what happens when the transition from earth to eternity takes place. However, there have been countless near-death experiences which contain quite similar reports. They include descriptions of long tunnels, a bright light, a feeling of peacefulness, and meeting up with loved ones already on the other side. One thing that has always interested me is whether spiritual growth is still possible right up until the last second of our crossover. Many people arrive at a point when they give up on making shifts spiritually and otherwise. On April 27, 2023, 1 took that question into my morning meditation with The Holy Spirit. I discerned this response: "It is not the 'Quantity'" of the time remaining, but the "Quality". Soul growth is possible right up to the moment of transition. So many people think: "I'm done. It's too late to change my spiritual behavior." Nothing could be further from the truth. You can still be growing your soul as you ascend to God's Kingdom. It is never too late for forgiveness and healing. Spectacular examples of both are available right until the last possible moment. Believe in the limitless possibilities that still lurk in the final few minutes of human existence. Individuals can often hold on to long grudges until right before the end. Try to rid yourself of all thoughts of animosity, anger and revenge. Negative emotions are not allowed to travel with you into Heaven. Shed them all before the final journey begins. God realizes that the concept of releasing everything is hard to accept. You should see how some people cling to their material possessions! Mortal conditioning is so different from spiritual reality. You never need to interact with your tormentors again. When you enter God's Kingdom, everything becomes goodness and Light. Here is the best thing about the positive nature of eternity. It lasts forever."

BACK TO MY SOUL'S
FIRST DAY IN HEAVEN

As I stood amidst the throng that had come out
to greet me, I felt no sadness about leaving the
earth. The last few months of my human life
had been physically painful. I struggled hard
just to get from one place to another. I had never experienced mobility problems before. I felt
chained to my walker and a collection of canes.
I kept waiting for the inevitable fall that bedev-
ils the elderly. Thankfully, my Guardian Angels
kept me upright. But I was close to toppling
over on several occasions. In meditation, I kept
hearing "Take it slow!" Good advice for the fee-
ble.

My newly arrived soul turned to my dear wife
and asked: "What happens now?" "Good question," she answered. "I can answer in terms of
human time. However, remember, there are no
hours or minutes up here. Eternity just keeps
evolving. You will hear a lot about the wonders
of Heaven. Just try to let it all unfold naturally.
Everything will fall into place. I do want to
share one of our best attributes. You are free to
travel anywhere and visit any place. There is a

realistic replica of the entire human world available to you. If you have ever wanted to stand at the top of Mount Everest and survey the earth below, just schedule it. If you ever yearned to sit in the audience of a Mozart concert, no problem. There is almost always a new Shakespeare production opening somewhere in Heaven. New arrivals grow our playlist every day. You and I never made it up to the Grand Canyon when we did church in Sun City. It was one of the first places I visited after my soul arrived here. What beauty and grandeur! It is still one of my favorites. You can also schedule one-on-one meetings with any soul. Of course, another beautiful thing is the freedom of choice to say "no" to anybody that desires to see you. Get-togethers are never coerced. Either party can opt out of a soul-to-soul experience with no explanation. There are no appeals. Remember, Heaven is all about peace and harmony. That especially includes not wanting to see certain family members. Since there is no guilt, there are no guilty feelings to process."

"What about famous people?" my soul inquired. "I've always wanted to meet Winston Churchill". "All you have to do is ask," Jan's soul replied. "All he can say is no. I hear Mr. Churchill always has a full calendar of appointments." I did feel overwhelmed, just by the first things I was hearing about Heaven. "Do you mean there are no downsides?" I asked. "No rain, " she quickly offered.

Just then, I felt a warm and joyful presence near
me. When I questioned Jan's soul regarding the
phenomenon, she said: "Oh, that's just Thelma.
She is here to show you around. Thelma is one
of the Super Guides. You are lucky to get her."
"Why is that?" I inquired. "Thelma is a charac-
ter. She's full of jokes. Trust me." "So, this Thelma was a woman in her earthly life?", I asked.
"Oh, she was a female many times in her incar-
nations. Like every soul, Thelma has lived before
as both a male and a female persona. In truth,
she has quite a few more male lives under her
belt. Several were spent during the decline and
fall of the Roman Empire living it up. Theolo-
nius (as he was known then) worked for Nero
during the burning of Rome. He was also pres-
ent on the night the crazy emperor killed himself. Anyway, Thelma's female soul got the
charm. You will enjoy being around her."

Just then, I felt a teasing laugh in my vicinity.
"Oh, dear Lord, not another Texan," it said.
"What have I done to deserve this? Anyway, I
am here to answer any questions and give you a
quick tour of where you will be spending eternity. I know you just arrived and must be con-
fused. Any burning questions off the top? Go for
it. Ask me anything."

"Is there a Hell?" I offered. "Well, you don't
waste any time on subtleties," She (Him or it)
commented. "Here is the answer," Thelma said.
"Most of the 'Hell'" situations are created by you
while you are living out your human life. Anyone

falling prey to addictions knows what I mean. That is all erased when you get here. I am sure you do understand that the current population of Hell consists of fallen angels. They couldn't or wouldn't abide by the sacred rules of God's Kingdom. It takes a lot to get kicked out of Heaven. But evil exists. The Principalities of Darkness and Separation from God enjoy creating trouble for human beings. They are riding high now. The world is on a downward spiral. Porn, gambling, drugs, you name it. I am not sure how things will end for the human contingent. Of course, God always triumphs in the end. Even when it rained and poured for 40 days and nights, Spirit selected a remnant and kept them safe in an ark. If necessary, something like that (but not a flood) could happen again. Of course, God has more tools available to salvage a remnant this time, like rocket ships. No more crowded arks. Man, did those animals stink!"

"So, Satan really exists?" I ventured. "Absolutely," Thelma replied. "But here is a new piece of information. There have been more than a dozen different Devils since Lucifer fell out of favor with God. There is a constant power struggle taking place in the Underworld. Everyone is vying for attention. Right now, as I said, the porn, gambling and drug czars are leading the way. It's hard to know who's ahead from one day to the next. Humans are so fickle with their addictions and foibles. For a long time, everything revolved around 'money'. But cash and things are so passe now. Wealth is ubiquitous. Everybody has it, so people are going for different ways to corrupt and separate themselves from God." "Politics" is also coming on strong. That is always the #1 objective *for* evil doers, separating humans from their Maker.

"So, even bad people get a crack at Heaven?" "Of course," Thelma replied. "Believe you me, 99.99 percent want no part of their previously tangled and unhappy lives. They find Nirvana when they arrive here. There is no desire to go back into any kind of human unhappiness. That is especially true of anyone experiencing any type of abuse.

"What is the best thing about eternity?" I queried "Thelma". Without hesitation, she answered, "Time is the best feature. There is 'time' to do anything and everything. The phrase "'Just hurry up and do it' stays forever non-existent. It takes a while for Type A human beings to adjust, but most of them grasp the concept without too much resistance."

"Anything else stands out besides 'time'"? I inquired. "Most everyone loves the peacefulness around here," Thelma's soul replied. "Many souls have led hard and challenging lives. They are usually the happiest souls in Heaven. Also, any spirit that dealt with physical pain (such as both you and Jan) is grateful for the end of suffering. That is one reason that so many human beings wish for death at the end. It is a big-time relief." "What about reincarnation?" I probed. "Does it mean I must go right back to earth in some other form?" "No," Thelma responded, emphatically. "In fact, my dear one, most souls do not go back. There are two types that return most often. If someone was on the verge of completing an important spiritual project, that soul might go back to wrap it up. The other most common type is some misguided spirit that still has big-time amends to make. There are not as many of those cases, but it does happen. Pedophiles, war criminals and those who traffic in other human beings are all examples of soul tyrants. I think you will be in Heaven for a while before you might be offered the chance to return. I personally see you moving forward up here. I would sponsor you myself as an angel in training. Just stay open for spiritual service in eternity. I find it quite gratifying. I think you would enjoy the 'wings' that go with it."

"Who is really in charge up here?" I questioned. "You know how we human beings like structure." Thelma paused before answering. "Well," she finally responded, "Everybody and nobody. Except for God and His closest archangels, we are all equal in The Creator's view. "Bosses" are all remnants of the material world. No one in Heaven is vying to get ahead. We did that on Earth. Up here, everyone already has it made in the shade drinking lemonade. Competing for personal glory was then, now is now. We are all living in real Glory. Nothing is better than what we have right here, right now. You'll see."

"What about those zillionaires and billionaires that come here without their money?" I inquired.

"It must be hard for them, becoming just like everyone else." I felt Thelma's spirit warming up to the question. "You might be surprised to know that many rich people are relieved by not having the responsibility that comes with wealth. For one thing, there are no more questions about the motivation of others. On the mortal scene, it can be tough knowing who your true friends are. Ask anyone who possessed money and then lost it. It can get lonesome real fast. The same thing can be true with fame. Being publicly recognized comes and goes. These former 'stars' can be some of the most unhappy human beings. Think about it. People are praising your name one minute, cursing you out the next, and then just ignoring you. Egotistical human beings are asking for it. What goes around really does come around. Of course, Satan loves corrupting anyone seeking fame and fortune. They are by far the easiest marks."

I felt Thelma's soul wanting to switch things around. "Now, let me query you for a while," she mused. "Would it surprise you to know that most all of the things you worried about on Earth had no real meaning?" "What are you referring to specifically," I countered. "Oh, little things like whether your team won on Sunday. Many human beings live and die with their sports teams. It is a harmless diversion and, personally, I've always been a Packer's fan. Lately I've been rooting for the Eagles, especially over your Cowboys. But, in the totality of what's important, it really doesn't matter. There is always a new season, with new faces."

"So, what are the truly important things on earth?" I asked. "Oh, there are so many," Thelma's soul reflected. "However, most of them get ignored. Just being kind to others brings happiness and fulfillment. More people should try it. Forgiveness is always good, it can relieve so much. You won't be happy if you constantly judge other folks. Nobody made you the foreman of a jury that enjoys coming down on others. "Minding your own business" is a worthy pursuit. Give up trying to control others. Control is one of human life's big illusions. Are you beginning to see how much time gets wasted by human beings in non-productive ways?"

"How do all of those bad habits get turned around in Heaven?" I ventured. Thelma responded: "You must understand this one thing about eternity. We represent the greatest effort imaginable in the field of Continuing Education. Heaven is the zenith in discovering knowledge. Souls grow in many ways. Gaining new awareness and insight stands as a magnificent way to evolve upward. The most hopeless human beings are those who proclaim: 'I've already learned all I need to know.' They are closed to new thoughts, different ideas and other ways to look at things. I feel bad for closed minds. Just remain open and receptive. You will do fine. Now, before we really begin the tour of Eternity, I want you to have one more word with your sweet Mother Edith and dear wife Jan. For now, I want to close with just 12 words that sum up everything: "Do not be afraid to live. Do not be afraid to die."

With that, I found myself again standing with my sweet mother Edith and dear wife Jan. I felt such warmth and acceptance. Mother spoke first: "Jan and I are glad you made it. So are your friends from over the years. We look forward to our soul life together in God's Kingdom. Believe me, the best is yet to come." Then, I felt Jan's angel wings wrapping around my newly arrived form. "You're finally home, Allie, you are finally home." "And I was."

NOT THE END,
ONLY THE BEGINNING

Rev. Allen C. Liles is the author of Sitting With God: Meditating for God's Divine Guidance, Exodus 20: The Ten Commandments, Luke 15: The Prodigal Son, John 14: The Most Important Book in the New Testament, Ephesians 6: Putting on the Whole Armor of God, Daniel 6: Surviving the Lion's Den, and Psalm 23: Trusting God in All Things, plus other spiritual writings. All books are available on Amazon.com and other online booksellers.

www.ingramcontent.com/pod-product-compliance
Lightning Source LLC
Chambersburg PA
CBHW071757020426
42331CB00008B/2316